ARTIFICIAL INTELLIGENCE

A SIMPLE GUIDE TO BOOSTING BUSINESS PROFITS

DANIEL DESTA

CONTENTS

PREFACE

Welcome to "Artificial Intelligence: A Simple Guide to Boosting Business Profits." In today's rapidly evolving world, technology is playing an increasingly important role in the success of businesses. One of the most exciting and innovative technologies that is revolutionizing the business world is artificial intelligence (AI). AI has the potential to transform the way businesses operate, making them more efficient, productive, and profitable. However, many business owners and managers are still unsure about how AI works and how it can benefit their organizations. That's where this book comes in. We aim to provide you with a simple and straightforward guide to AI and how it can help boost your business profits.

PROLOGUE

In this fast-paced and ever-changing world, businesses must keep up with the latest technologies to remain competitive. AI has been a game-changer for many industries, from healthcare to finance to retail. AI can help businesses make better decisions, improve customer experiences, and streamline operations. However, many business owners and managers are hesitant to adopt AI due to a lack of understanding or fear of the unknown. This book is designed to demystify AI and provide practical advice on how to implement AI in your business to maximize profits and stay ahead of the curve.

FOREWORD

As a business owner and AI enthusiast, I am thrilled to introduce "Artificial Intelligence: A Simple Guide to Boosting Business Profits." This book is an excellent resource for anyone who wants to understand the basics of AI and how it can benefit their business. The author has done an outstanding job of explaining complex concepts in simple terms, making it accessible to anyone, regardless of their technical background. This book provides real-world examples and practical advice on how to implement AI in your business to increase profitability. I highly recommend this book to anyone who wants to stay ahead of the competition and take their business to the next level with AI.

—Dr. Melania Flores

CHAPTER 1

INTRODUCTION TO AI IN BUSINESS: FROM BUZZWORD TO GAME-CHANGER

Dear fellow business owners,

We all know the struggle of running a successful business. Whether it's keeping up with the latest trends, managing a team of employees, or juggling finances, there's always something to keep us up at night.

But what if I told you that there was a way to revolutionize your business and make all those struggles a little bit easier? Yes, my friends, I'm talking about AI, or artificial intelligence.

Now, before you start picturing a dystopian future where robots have taken over your business, let me explain. AI isn't about replacing human employees, but rather augmenting their abilities and making their jobs easier.

For example, imagine if you could automate your customer service with a chatbot that could answer common questions and free up your employees to handle more complex inquiries. Or, what if you could use AI to analyze data and make better-informed decisions about which products to stock or which marketing campaigns to invest in?

These are just a few of the many ways that AI can revolutionize your business. But why should you care? Well, for starters, AI can help you save time and money. By automating repetitive tasks and analyzing data more efficiently, you can free up your employees to focus on more important things, like growing your business.

Let's begin by first knowing exactly what AI is.

Artificial Intelligence (AI) has been around for decades but has only in recent years started to make a real impact on businesses. No longer just a buzzword, AI is quickly becoming a game-changer for businesses of all sizes. In this chapter, we'll explore the definition of AI, its impact on businesses, and why it's becoming increasingly important for modern businesses. We'll also look at the future of AI in business management and the potential it holds for shaping the way businesses operate.

1. Definition of AI and its impact on businesses

AI is a branch of computer science that deals with creating machines that can perform tasks that would normally require human intelligence. This includes tasks such as recognizing patterns, learning from experience, making predictions, and making decisions. The goal of AI is to create machines that can think and act like humans.

The impact of AI on businesses has been profound. It's enabling businesses to automate many of the manual tasks that are time-consuming and error-prone, such as data entry and analysis. AI is also providing businesses with valuable insights and predictions based on large amounts of data. This is leading to increased efficiency, improved customer experiences, and increased profits.

But that's just the tip of the iceberg. AI is also keeping businesses ahead of the competition by providing them with a competitive advantage. For example, AI-powered customer service can help businesses provide faster and more accurate responses to customer inquiries, leading to increased customer satisfaction. AI can also help businesses identify new opportunities and make better decisions, leading to increased efficiency and profitability.

2. Importance of AI in modern businesses

The importance of AI in modern businesses cannot be overstated. With the vast amounts of data being generated every day, businesses need a way to make sense of it all and extract valuable insights. AI provides a solution to this problem by enabling businesses to process and analyze vast amounts of data in real-time.

In addition, AI is helping businesses stay ahead of the curve by providing them with a competitive advantage. Businesses that embrace AI can automate many of their manual tasks, make better decisions, and provide better customer experiences. This is leading to increased efficiency, improved customer satisfaction, and increased profits.

But the impact of AI goes beyond just increased efficiency and profits. AI is also helping businesses stay relevant in an ever-changing business landscape. Businesses that fail to embrace AI risk being left behind as AI becomes more widespread and its applications become more sophisticated.

3. The future of AI in business management

The future of AI in business management is bright and holds immense potential for businesses of all sizes. As AI continues to evolve, it will enable businesses to automate more tasks, make better decisions, and provide better customer experiences. It will also lead to the creation of new business models and industries that are based on AI and its applications.

For example, AI has the potential to revolutionize the way we think about customer service. Instead of waiting on hold for hours to speak with a customer service representative, customers will be able to use AI-powered chatbots to get the answers they need in real-time. This will lead to increased customer satisfaction.

AI also has the ability to change the way we think about product development and innovation. By analyzing vast amounts of data, AI can help businesses identify new opportunities and make better decisions. This will lead to the creation of new products and services that meet the needs of customers in innovative and unexpected ways.

AI is set to play a major role in shaping the future of business management, and businesses that embrace it will reap the benefits. The potential of AI is only limited by our imagination, and it's up to us to think creatively about how we can use AI to transform the way we do business.

In the coming chapters, we'll explore how businesses can implement AI in their operations and how they can leverage AI to improve their processes, increase efficiency, and stay ahead of the competition. We'll look at the different types of AI, such as machine learning and deep learning, and how they can be applied in different areas of business, such as marketing, sales, and customer service.

I'm also including an appendix detailing several AI solutions that have proven helpful for countless businesses like yours.

So, whether you're a small business owner or a Fortune 500 CEO, this book is designed to help you understand how you can use AI to transform your business and stay ahead of the competition. By the end of this book, you'll have a clear understanding of the impact of AI on business, the importance of AI in modern businesses, and the future of AI in business management.

CHAPTER 2

AI-POWERED DECISIONS: A GAME-CHANGER IN BUSINESS STRATEGY

When it comes to making decisions, there's nothing quite like having a solid understanding of the data behind it. In the world of business, having access to accurate data is crucial for making informed decisions that drive growth and success. However, collecting and analyzing data can be a time-consuming and complex process. That's where AI comes in.

In this chapter, we'll dive into how AI is revolutionizing the way businesses make decisions and how it's becoming an increasingly important tool in today's fast-paced business landscape.

1. Understanding the Role of AI in Decision-Making

One of the biggest advantages of AI is its ability to process vast amounts of data in a short amount of time. By analyzing patterns and trends in data, AI can help businesses make informed decisions based on evidence-based insights. This not only saves time but also improves the accuracy of decisions, as AI is able to identify key trends and insights that may not be immediately visible to humans.

2. Using AI to Analyze Data and Make Informed Decisions

AI can be used in a variety of ways to improve decision-making in businesses. For example, it can be used to analyze customer data to understand buying patterns and preferences, which can then be used to inform marketing and sales strategies. Additionally, AI can be used to analyze financial data to help businesses make informed decisions about investments and spending.

One of the most exciting applications of AI in decision-making is its ability to predict future trends and outcomes. For example, by analyzing data from past sales, AI can help businesses make informed decisions about inventory levels and stock management. This can help businesses avoid overstocking, which can lead to waste, and ensure they have enough stock on hand to meet customer demand.

3. Integrating AI into Your Business Strategy and Operations

To truly realize the benefits of AI in decision-making, it's important to integrate it into your business strategy and operations. This can involve incorporating AI into your existing processes and systems, or it can involve building new processes and systems specifically designed to support AI.

Regardless of the approach you choose, it's important to work with a team of experts who understand the technology and can help you effectively implement it. This could mean working with AI developers, data scientists, or business consultants, depending on the needs of your business.

AI is revolutionizing the way businesses make decisions. By processing vast amounts of data and analyzing patterns and trends, AI can help businesses make informed decisions based on evidence-based insights. This not only saves time but also improves the accuracy of decisions, as AI is able to identify key trends and insights that may not be immediately visible to humans.

By integrating AI into your business strategy and operations, you can leverage its full potential and make data-driven decisions that drive growth and success. However, it's important to work with a team of experts who understand the technology and can help you effectively implement it. With AI, the future of decision-making in business is brighter and more promising than ever before.

CHAPTER 3

OPTIMIZING AI FOR INCREASED EFFICIENCY

With its ability to process vast amounts of data, automate repetitive tasks and processes, and improve customer experience, AI is helping businesses become more efficient and effective in their operations. In this chapter, we'll explore how AI is revolutionizing business efficiency by reducing costs, increasing profitability, and optimizing processes.

AUTOMATING REPETITIVE TASKS AND PROCESSES

One of the biggest advantages of AI is its ability to automate repetitive tasks and processes. By eliminating manual and time-consuming activities, AI can free up employees to focus on more high-value tasks and projects. From data entry and customer service to financial analysis and inventory management, AI can automate a wide range of business functions, improving productivity and freeing up resources for other areas of the business.

- AI-powered automation can free up employees from repetitive and time-consuming tasks, allowing them to focus on more high-value work.
- AI can automate a wide range of business functions, from customer service and data entry to financial analysis and inventory management.
- By eliminating manual and time-consuming activities, AI can help businesses become more productive and efficient, freeing up resources for other areas of the business.

Some specific AI tools that are affective in this department include Akkio.com & Excelformulabot.com. I've included a rundown of each of these tools at the end.

IMPROVING CUSTOMER EXPERIENCE WITH AI-POWERED SOLUTIONS

AI can also be used to improve customer experience by providing personalized and relevant solutions. From chatbots that assist with customer service to AI-powered recommendations based on individual preferences, AI can help businesses build better relationships with their customers. This not only improves customer satisfaction but also helps businesses stay ahead of the competition by offering innovative and engaging customer experiences.

- AI can help improve customer experience by providing personalized and relevant solutions.

- AI-powered chatbots can assist with customer service and answer customer questions, improving response times and overall customer satisfaction.
- By using AI to understand individual customer preferences, businesses can make more targeted and relevant recommendations, helping to build stronger relationships with customers.

REDUCING COSTS AND INCREASING PROFITABILITY THROUGH AI

Finally, AI can help businesses reduce costs and increase profitability by streamlining processes and improving efficiency. By automating repetitive tasks and processes, AI can help businesses reduce labor costs and improve productivity. Additionally, AI-powered solutions can help businesses identify inefficiencies and waste, which can then be addressed to improve cost-effectiveness.

- AI can help businesses reduce costs and increase profitability by streamlining processes and improving efficiency.
- AI-powered automation can reduce labor costs and improve productivity, helping businesses to operate more effectively and efficiently.
- AI can help identify inefficiencies and waste, allowing businesses to improve cost-effectiveness and maximize their bottom line.

We've explored the many ways that AI can be optimized for increased efficiency. From automating repetitive tasks and processes, to improving the customer experience with AI-powered solutions, to reducing costs and increasing profitability through AI, the potential benefits are endless. However, it's important to remember that AI is not a one-size-fits-all solution. Each company must carefully consider their unique needs and goals before implementing AI solutions. The key to success is finding the right balance between human intuition and AI algorithms.

AI has the potential to revolutionize the way we do business, but it's up to us to make the most of its capabilities. By carefully considering your goals, automating repetitive tasks, improving the customer experience, and reducing costs, you can unlock the full potential of AI and create a more efficient, profitable, and customer-focused future.

CHAPTER 4

UTILIZING AI FOR BETTER CUSTOMER ENGAGEMENT

Let's delve into another exciting area of AI innovation: customer engagement. Whether you're a small business or a large corporation, improving customer engagement is essential to your long-term success. Here's how AI can help you achieve this goal.

UNDERSTANDING CUSTOMER BEHAVIOR AND PREFERENCES

To engage with customers effectively, you need to understand their behaviors and preferences. This includes understanding what they want, what they need, and what they expect from your brand. AI can help you gather this information using predictive analytics. Predictive analytics involves analyzing customer data to identify patterns and trends. This information can then be used to make informed decisions about how to engage with your customers. For example, you can use AI to determine which products are most popular with your customers and target your marketing efforts accordingly.

Programs such as Promo, Jasper, and Albert.ai are great tools for marketing purposes; see the appendix at the end for more in-depth details.

PERSONALIZING CUSTOMER EXPERIENCES WITH AI

Personalization is key to effective customer engagement. By personalizing customer experiences, you show your customers that you understand their needs and preferences. AI makes this process much easier. For example, AI can be used to analyze customer data and suggest products or services that they might be interested in. This can be done through the use of recommendation algorithms. Additionally, AI can be used to create personalized messages that are tailored to each customer's individual needs. This can help to improve customer satisfaction and increase the likelihood of repeat business.

IMPROVING CUSTOMER SATISFACTION AND LOYALTY THROUGH AI

Finally, AI can be used to improve customer satisfaction and loyalty. This can be done by providing customers with quick and effective customer service. AI-powered chatbots are a great example of this. Chatbots can provide customers with instant answers to their questions, reducing wait times and improving the overall customer experience. Additionally, AI can be used to analyze customer feedback and provide insights into areas where improvements can be made. This can help to ensure that your customers are happy with your products and services, which is essential to building customer loyalty.

AI has the potential to revolutionize customer engagement. By understanding customer behavior and preferences, personalizing customer experiences, and improving customer satisfaction and loyalty, you can use AI to create a more engaging and fulfilling customer experience. Whether you're a small business or a large corporation, incorporating AI into your customer engagement strategy is a must in today's digital age. Embrace the power of AI and start enhancing your customer engagement today!

CHAPTER 5

UNDERSTANDING THE CHALLENGES OF AI IMPLEMENTATION: BREAKING DOWN BARRIERS AND OVERCOMING OBSTACLES

In our fast-paced world, businesses are constantly looking for ways to stay ahead of the competition and improve their operations. AI has emerged as a powerful tool that can help businesses achieve these goals, but the road to AI implementation can be a bumpy one.

In this chapter, we'll explore the challenges of AI implementation and how businesses can overcome them. Let's dive into the three key challenges:

1. **Resistance to change from employees and stakeholders:** One of the biggest obstacles to AI implementation is resistance from employees and stakeholders. When change is proposed, people tend to get uncomfortable, and the introduction of AI can be no different.

Employees may worry about job security, and stakeholders may worry about the impact on profits.

However, by educating employees and stakeholders about the benefits of AI, businesses can help to reduce resistance to change. Companies can also implement change management strategies to help employees adjust to the new technology, such as training programs and communication plans.

2. **Technical limitations and data privacy concerns:** Another challenge of AI implementation is the technical limitations and data privacy concerns that come with the use of AI. Companies must ensure that their systems are up to date and that their data is secure. They must also make sure that the data they collect is used in an ethical manner and complies with privacy regulations.

To overcome these challenges, companies must invest in the right technology and infrastructure, as well as put in place robust data privacy policies and procedures. They should also work with trusted partners who have a proven track record in delivering secure and compliant AI solutions.

3. **Cost and time required for AI implementation:** Finally, cost and time are often cited as major barriers to AI implementation. Implementing AI can be expensive, and it can also take a significant amount of time to get it up and running.

However, businesses can overcome these challenges by prioritizing their AI initiatives and investing in solutions that offer the greatest ROI. They can also break down large AI projects into smaller, more manageable phases, and they can explore alternative financing options, such as cloud-based solutions that offer more cost-effective and flexible options.

The challenges of AI implementation are significant, but they are not insurmountable. By understanding these challenges and taking a proactive approach to overcome them, businesses can successfully implement AI and reap the benefits it offers. In the next chapter, we'll explore the different types of AI and how they can be applied in different areas of business.

CHAPTER 6

PREPARING YOUR BUSINESS FOR AI IMPLEMENTATION: TAKING THE FIRST STEP TOWARDS TRANSFORMATION

Now that you understand the challenges of AI implementation, it's time to start preparing your business for the transformation. Let's take a closer look at how you can get your business ready for AI, from assessing your business to planning the implementation process and setting goals.

1. **Assessing the current state of your business:** The first step in preparing your business for AI is to assess the current state of your operations. This includes evaluating your technology infrastructure, data management practices, and overall business processes. By understanding your business's strengths and weaknesses, you can identify areas where AI can bring the most value.

2. **Identifying areas where AI can bring value:** Once you have a good understanding of your business's current state, it's time to start identifying areas where AI can bring the most value. This may include improving customer service, streamlining operations, or increasing sales. It's important to prioritize these areas and focus on the ones that will have the biggest impact on your business.

3. **Planning the implementation process and setting goals:** With a clear understanding of your business's current state and areas where AI can bring value, it's time to start planning the implementation process and setting goals. This includes developing a detailed implementation plan, determining the resources you'll need, and establishing clear goals and metrics to measure success.

To ensure a successful AI implementation, it's important to work with a team of experts who have experience in AI and business management. This may include data scientists, AI developers, and business consultants. They can help you develop a customized plan that considers the unique needs and goals of your business.

In addition to working with experts, it's also important to involve key stakeholders in the implementation process. This includes employees, customers, and partners. By involving them in the process, you can ensure that everyone is on board and understands the benefits of AI.

Finally, it's important to be flexible and open to change. The AI landscape is rapidly evolving, and new solutions and technologies are emerging all the time. By being open to change, you can ensure that your business is always on the cutting edge of AI innovation.

Preparing your business for AI implementation is a critical step in the transformation process. By assessing the current state of your business, identifying areas where AI can bring value, and planning the implementation process and setting goals, you can ensure that your AI implementation is successful and that your business reaps the benefits of this powerful technology.

CHAPTER 7

FINDING THE RIGHT AI SOLUTION FOR YOUR BUSINESS: NAVIGATING THE AI LANDSCAPE

Now that you've prepared your business for AI implementation, it's time to start looking for the right AI solution for your business. How can you find the right AI solution that meets your need?

1. **Understanding the different types of AI:** The first step in finding the right AI solution for your business is to understand the different types of AI. There are several different types of AI, including machine learning, natural language processing, computer vision, and deep learning. Each type of AI is designed to address specific challenges and opportunities, and it's important to understand the differences between them to ensure that you choose the right solution for your business.

2. **Evaluating the capabilities of AI solutions and vendors:** Once you have a good understanding of the different types of AI, it's time to start evaluating the capabilities of AI solutions and vendors. This includes reviewing product features, performance metrics, and customer testimonials. It's also important to consider the vendor's experience and expertise in AI, as well as their track record of delivering successful AI implementations.

3. **Choosing the right AI solution for your business:** With a clear understanding of the different types of AI and the capabilities of AI solutions and vendors, it's time to start choosing the right AI solution for your business. To make the right choice, it's important to consider your business goals and objectives, as well as your budget and timeline. You should also consider the compatibility of the solution with your existing technology infrastructure, as well as the level of support and training that the vendor provides.

It's also important to consider the impact of AI on your business culture and work processes. Will the AI solution complement and enhance your existing work processes, or will it disrupt them? Will employees embrace the new technology, or will they resist it? These are important questions to consider when choosing the right AI solution for your business.

Finally, it's important to take a phased approach to AI implementation. Start with a small pilot project and build from there. This will help you refine your implementation strategy and make any necessary adjustments along the way.

Finding the right AI solution for your business requires a thoughtful and deliberate approach. By understanding the different types of AI, evaluating the capabilities of AI solutions and vendors, and choosing the right AI solution for your business, you can ensure that your AI implementation is a success and that your business reaps the benefits of this powerful technology.

CHAPTER 8

BUILDING A STRONG AI TEAM: ASSEMBLING THE RIGHT PLAYERS FOR THE GAME

Implementing AI in your business is not a one-person job. It requires a team of experts with a diverse set of skills and expertise to ensure that your AI implementation is successful. In this chapter, we'll look at how you can build a strong AI team to drive your AI initiatives forward.

1. **Understanding the skills and expertise required for AI implementation**: The first step in building a strong AI team is to understand the skills and expertise required for AI implementation. This includes data scientists, software engineers, business analysts, and project managers. You need to understand the specific skills and expertise required for each role, as well as the level of experience and training required, to ensure that you have the right people on your team.

2. **Building an internal AI team or outsourcing to experts:** Once you understand the skills and expertise required for AI implementation, you need to decide whether you want to build an internal AI team or outsource to experts. Building an internal AI team can be more cost-effective, but it requires significant investments in training and development, as well as ongoing support and maintenance. Outsourcing to experts can be more expensive, but it provides access to a wider pool of talent and expertise, as well as the ability to tap into the latest technologies and methodologies.

3. **Training and educating employees on AI and its applications:** Regardless of whether you build an internal AI team or outsource to experts, it's important to provide training and education to all employees on AI and its applications. This includes understanding how AI is transforming the business landscape, as well as the benefits and challenges of AI implementation. It's also important to provide training on the specific AI tools and technologies that your team will be using, as well as any new work processes and procedures that will be introduced because of AI implementation.

Building a strong AI team is crucial to the success of your AI implementation. By understanding the skills and expertise required for AI implementation, building an internal AI team, or outsourcing to experts, and providing training and education to employees on AI and its applications, you can ensure that you have the right people and resources in place to drive your AI initiatives forward.

CHAPTER 9

INTEGRATING AI INTO YOUR BUSINESS PROCESSES: PLUGGING AI INTO THE MACHINE

As companies look to harness the power of AI to drive growth and improve efficiency, it's essential to have a clear plan in place for integrating this technology into existing processes. The goal of this chapter is to help you understand the key steps to streamline AI integration into your business processes, maximize its impact and ensure a smooth implementation.

ASSESSING THE IMPACT OF AI ON CURRENT PROCESSES

The first step in integrating AI into your business processes is to assess the impact it will have on existing operations. This involves understanding how AI will interact with current systems and processes, identifying areas that may need to be modified, and considering how AI will impact the workforce. To ensure a smooth transition, it's important to conduct a thorough impact assessment that considers the following factors:

- Workflow: Evaluate how AI will impact existing workflows and identify any bottlenecks or challenges that need to be addressed.
- Employee impact: Consider the impact AI will have on employees and determine whether they will need to be retrained or reallocated to different roles.
- Technical infrastructure: Evaluate the technical infrastructure required to support AI and identify any gaps that need to be filled.
- Data privacy: Ensure that data privacy and security measures are in place to protect sensitive information and comply with regulations.

DEFINING NEW PROCESSES AND PROCEDURES FOR AI INTEGRATION

Once you have assessed the impact of AI on your business processes, the next step is to define new processes and procedures that will be required for successful integration. This may involve modifying existing processes, creating new ones, or completely overhauling your business model. When defining new processes, consider the following factors:

- Goals and objectives: Identify the specific goals and objectives you want to achieve through AI integration, such as greater efficiency, increased revenue, or improved customer experience.
- Workflow: Define how AI will interact with existing workflows and processes and determine how it will impact employees.
- Roles and responsibilities: Clearly define the roles and responsibilities of each team member involved in the AI integration process.

- Performance metrics: Define metrics to measure the success of AI integration, such as efficiency gains, customer satisfaction, and revenue increases.

IMPLEMENTING AI AND MONITORING ITS PERFORMANCE

The final step in integrating AI into your business processes is to implement the technology and monitor its performance. This involves deploying AI systems, training employees, and continuously monitoring the technology to ensure it is delivering the desired results. To ensure a successful implementation, consider the following factors:

- Employee training: Provide employees with the necessary training and support to effectively use AI systems.
- Performance monitoring: Continuously monitor the performance of AI systems, and adjust processes and procedures as needed to optimize results.
- User feedback: Encourage users to provide feedback on the performance of AI systems and use this information to continuously improve the technology.
- Data quality: Ensure that data inputs are accurate, up-to-date, and of high quality to ensure the best possible results from AI systems.

The integration of AI into business processes is a crucial step in harnessing the full potential of this technology. It requires careful planning, assessment, and execution to ensure a seamless and successful integration. The key to success is to approach AI implementation with a well-thought-out plan and to focus on streamlining the process.

One way to streamline the implementation process is to focus on automating manual and repetitive tasks. This not only saves time and resources, but it also eliminates human error and improves overall efficiency. Additionally, it is important to continuously monitor and evaluate the performance of AI systems to identify areas for improvement and optimize their effectiveness.

Another way to streamline the implementation process is to involve all relevant stakeholders in the planning and execution stages. This helps to ensure that everyone is aware of the goals and objectives, and that everyone understands the role they play in the implementation process. Effective communication and collaboration between stakeholders are essential to ensuring that everyone is on the same page and working towards the same goals.

Finally, it is important to keep in mind that AI implementation is an ongoing process that requires regular attention and maintenance. This means that businesses must be prepared to continuously invest in their AI systems and processes to keep up with evolving technology and changing business needs.

The integration of AI into business processes is a complex and challenging process, but one that can bring significant benefits to businesses. By approaching AI implementation with a well-thought-out plan, focusing on streamlining the process, and continuously monitoring and improving performance, businesses can harness the full potential of AI and stay ahead of the competition.

CHAPTER 10

MANAGING AND MAINTAINING YOUR AI SYSTEM: KEEP YOUR MACHINE LEARNING MODEL IN SHAPE

Congratulations! You've made it to the final stretch. You've assessed your business, chosen the right AI solution, built a strong team, and successfully integrated AI into your processes. But now comes the most critical part of the journey - managing and maintaining your AI system. As with any technology, there will be challenges that arise. But with the right approach, you can ensure that your AI system continues to run smoothly and provide value to your business. Let's take a closer look at how to keep your AI system on track.

ENSURING DATA QUALITY AND ACCURACY

One of the most critical aspects of AI is the quality of the data it uses to make decisions. If the data is inaccurate, the AI system's results will be flawed, and it won't provide the desired outcomes. To avoid this, it's essential to establish processes and procedures for data collection, storage, and analysis. Regular data audits can help ensure that your data is accurate, complete, and up to date.

MONITORING PERFORMANCE AND MAKING NECESSARY ADJUSTMENTS

As your AI system processes data, it will generate results that you can use to assess its performance. By monitoring the performance metrics, you can identify areas where your AI system could be improved. This may involve adjusting the algorithms used, fine-tuning the data inputs, or changing the processes used to implement AI. Regular monitoring and adjustments will help ensure that your AI system remains effective and provides value to your business.

UPDATING AND UPGRADING YOUR AI SYSTEM REGULARLY

Just like with any technology, AI systems evolve and improve over time. Regular updates and upgrades can help keep your AI system current and provide new features and capabilities. It's essential to stay on top of these updates and upgrades and to incorporate them into your AI system as soon as possible. This will ensure that your system remains effective and provides ongoing value to your business.

Updating and upgrading the AI system is an ongoing process that requires careful planning and execution. This can include incorporating new features and capabilities, as well as fixing bugs and resolving any technical issues that may arise. It is crucial to work with your AI solution provider to understand the recommended schedule for updates and upgrades and to plan accordingly.

Managing and maintaining your AI system is critical to its success and longevity. By following best practices and establishing protocols for data quality and accuracy, performance monitoring, and updates and upgrades, you can ensure that your AI system is delivering the desired results and providing maximum value to your business. Remember, an AI system is only as good as the data and processes it is built upon, so it is essential to keep these elements in check and to continuously improve and evolve your AI system to meet the changing needs of your business.

CHAPTER 11

OVERCOMING RESISTANCE TO CHANGE: EMBRACING THE FUTURE WITH AI

When it comes to implementing AI in a business, one of the biggest challenges can be overcoming resistance to change from employees and stakeholders. After all, the implementation of AI means that there will be changes to the way the business operates, and these changes can be seen as a threat to the status quo. But with the right approach and proper communication, businesses can overcome this resistance and reap the rewards of AI implementation.

1. Communicating the Benefits of AI to Employees and Stakeholders

The first step in overcoming resistance to change is to communicate the benefits of AI to employees and stakeholders. This means clearly outlining what AI can bring to the table and how it can improve the business. For example, AI can increase efficiency, reduce costs, and provide more accurate and data-driven insights, which can ultimately lead to increased profitability.

When communicating the benefits of AI, it's important to be transparent and open about the changes that will be taking place. This includes explaining how AI will impact individual roles and what steps are being taken to support employees through this transition. It's also important to provide regular updates on the progress of the AI implementation and to solicit feedback from employees and stakeholders.

2. Addressing Concerns and Fears About AI

Another challenge to implementing AI is addressing concerns and fears about its impact. For example, some employees may worry that AI will automate their jobs or that it will lead to a loss of privacy. To overcome these fears, it's important to be transparent about how AI will be used and to provide reassurance that the implementation of AI is being done responsibly.

It's also important to address these fears head-on and provide employees with the information and resources they need to understand the positive impact AI can have. This can include training programs, regular meetings, and opportunities for employees to ask questions and provide feedback.

3. Building a Culture of Innovation and Embracing Change

Finally, to overcome resistance to change and fully embrace the future with AI, it's important to build a culture of innovation and change within your business. This means encouraging employees to be open-minded and willing to embrace new technologies and processes.

One way to build this culture is to foster an environment of innovation by creating opportunities for employees to experiment with new technologies, hosting brainstorming sessions and workshops, and encouraging employees to share their ideas and opinions.

Another way to build a culture of innovation is to celebrate successes and to recognize employees for their contributions. When employees see that their efforts are valued and appreciated, they are more likely to embrace new technologies and processes with excitement and enthusiasm.

Overcoming resistance to change is a critical component of successfully implementing AI in your business. By communicating the benefits of AI to employees and stakeholders, addressing their concerns and fears, and building a culture of innovation, you can help create a smooth transition for everyone involved.

It is important to remember that resistance to change is a natural response, but it can be mitigated through open and transparent communication. By engaging in active listening and taking steps to address any concerns that may arise, you can help build trust and buy-in from those who may be resistant.

In addition, investing in employee training and education can help build excitement and enthusiasm for AI and its potential. By empowering your employees with the knowledge and skills they need to succeed with AI, you can help them feel more confident in their abilities and more comfortable with the changes that are happening in the business.

Finally, it's crucial to stay committed to the process of change and be patient with those who may be struggling with the transition. By leading with empathy and demonstrating a willingness to work together, you can help build a stronger, more resilient, and more innovative business that is poised for success in the age of AI.

CHAPTER 12

THE FUTURE OF AI IN BUSINESS MANAGEMENT

As we reach the end of our journey through the wonders of AI in business management, it's time to turn our gaze to the horizon and consider what the future holds. The truth is, the future of AI is both exciting and uncertain, and it's important for businesses to stay ahead of the curve if they want to remain competitive. In this chapter, we'll explore some key ways in which businesses can prepare for the next wave of AI innovation.

First and foremost, it's essential to stay up to date on the latest advancements and trends in AI. This might mean regularly attending industry conferences, subscribing to relevant publications, or even collaborating with other businesses to share information and insights. By staying informed, you'll be able to identify opportunities for innovation and stay ahead of the curve.

It's also important to understand the potential for AI to shape the future of business. AI has already made a significant impact on various industries, from finance and healthcare to retail and manufacturing. And as AI continues to evolve, it will likely have an even greater impact in the future, transforming the way we work, live, and interact with one another.

One of the biggest trends in AI right now is the rise of autonomous systems. This refers to systems that can operate and make decisions independently, without human intervention. These systems are already being used in various industries, from self-driving cars to warehouse robots. As AI continues to evolve, it's likely that we'll see more and more autonomous systems in the future, changing the way we do business and challenging us to think about the role of humans in the workplace.

Another important trend in AI is the development of artificial general intelligence (AGI). This refers to AI systems that can perform any intellectual task that a human can. While AGI is still in its infancy, it has the potential to revolutionize the way we think about intelligence and consciousness.

As we look to the future of AI, it's important for businesses to consider the ethical and societal implications of these advancements. For example, as autonomous systems become more prevalent, we'll need to consider questions around job displacement and the impact on workers. We'll also need to consider questions around data privacy and the ethical use of AI.

The future of AI in business management is both exciting and uncertain. By staying up to date on advancements and trends, understanding the potential for AI to shape the future of business, and preparing for the next wave of AI innovation, businesses can position themselves for success in this rapidly changing landscape. So, let's embrace the future, stay curious, and continue to push the boundaries of what's possible with AI.

CHAPTER 13

BRINGING IT ALL TOGETHER

As we've seen throughout this book, AI is transforming the way we do business. From automating repetitive tasks to improving customer experiences and increasing profitability, the benefits of AI are countless. But as we near the end of this journey, it's worth taking a moment to reflect on what we've learned and where we're headed.

First and foremost, let's recap some of the key points we've covered:

- AI can automate repetitive tasks and processes, freeing up valuable time for employees to focus on more important tasks.
- By understanding customer behavior and preferences, businesses can personalize experiences and improve customer satisfaction and loyalty with AI-powered solutions.
- AI has the potential to reduce costs and increase profitability, making it an essential tool for businesses looking to stay competitive in today's market.

- To stay ahead of the curve, it's important to stay up to date on the latest AI advancements and trends.
- The future of AI is impossible to predict, but one thing is certain: it will continue to shape the way we do business and impact society in new and exciting ways.

With all of this in mind, what recommendations can we offer to businesses looking to implement AI?

First and foremost, it's crucial to have a clear understanding that AI is not a one-size-fits-all solution. It's important to understand the specific needs of your business and how AI can be used to meet those needs.

Additionally, it's important to have a plan in place for implementation. This may involve hiring new employees with AI expertise or partnering with an AI service provider. Whatever the case may be, having a clear plan in place will ensure a smooth and successful transition to AI.

Finally, it's crucial to stay ahead of the curve by staying informed on the latest AI advancements and trends. This will help ensure that your business remains competitive and relevant in the ever-evolving landscape of business and technology.

AI is no longer a futuristic concept, it's a real and tangible tool that businesses of all sizes can use to transform the way they do business. From automating tasks to improving customer experiences, the potential benefits of AI are immense. As we look to the future, it's important to embrace this technology and prepare for the next wave of AI innovation. With the right approach and a clear understanding of what AI can do, businesses can unlock its full potential and achieve new levels of success.

The future is in your hands....

AI TOOLS

Akkio.com

Pros and Cons of using www.akkio.com for business purposes compared to traditional ways that a business operates today:

Pros	Cons
Can automate and streamline business processes	Dependence on third-party software and technology
Provides real-time data analysis and insights	May require additional time and resources to set up
Can reduce errors and improve accuracy in decision-making	Limited ability to customize or tailor to specific needs
Offers a high level of scalability and flexibility	Requires additional cost for advanced features
Can enhance customer experience and satisfaction	Potential security concerns or data privacy risks

Using www.akkio.com for business purposes has several advantages. One of the most significant benefits is the ability to automate and streamline business processes. The platform can help businesses automate repetitive and time-consuming tasks, freeing up valuable time and resources for other business activities. Additionally, www.akkio.com provides real-time data analysis and insights, allowing businesses to make informed decisions and react quickly to changes in the market.

Another advantage of www.akkio.com is its ability to reduce errors and improve accuracy in decision-making. The platform's machine learning algorithms can help identify patterns and make predictions based on large data sets, improving the accuracy and reliability of business decisions. Additionally, www.akkio.com offers a high level of scalability and flexibility, making it a valuable tool for businesses of all sizes and industries.

However, there are some potential drawbacks to using www.akkio. com. One significant disadvantage is the dependence on third-party software and technology. The platform requires integration with other software and systems, which may require additional time and resources to set up. Additionally, www.akkio.com has limited customization capabilities, which may be a drawback for businesses with specific needs.

Another potential issue with www.akkio.com is the need for additional cost for advanced features. While the platform offers a range of tools and functionalities, some of the more advanced features may require an additional cost. This can be a significant expense for smaller businesses or startups.

Finally, there may be some security concerns or data privacy risks associated with using www.akkio.com. As a cloud-based service, www. akkio.com requires data to be stored off-site, which may be a concern for some businesses. It is essential to consider these potential risks and weigh them against the benefits of using the service.

Overall, www.akkio.com can be an effective tool for businesses looking to automate and streamline their processes, make informed decisions, and enhance the customer experience. However, it is essential to consider the potential drawbacks, such as dependence on third-party software and technology, limited customization capabilities, and potential security concerns, before deciding.

ALBERT.AI

Implementing Albert.ai into a business can be an excellent way to increase marketing productivity and efficiency compared to traditional marketing methods. By leveraging artificial intelligence and machine learning, Albert.ai can automate many marketing tasks, saving time and reducing human error. It can handle things like ad targeting, optimization, and analysis, leaving marketers more time to focus on strategy. This can lead to significant cost savings, especially for larger businesses with high marketing budgets.

One of the most significant advantages of Albert.ai is its ability to provide personalized marketing messages. By analyzing customer behavior and preferences, Albert.ai can create more targeted and relevant marketing messages that can increase engagement and conversion rates. The system can handle large-scale campaigns with ease, making it ideal for businesses that need to reach a wide audience.

Another significant benefit of Albert.ai is its real-time optimization capabilities. By adjusting campaigns in real-time based on performance metrics, Albert.ai can help businesses make data-driven decisions and optimize their marketing strategies. This can lead to more efficient spending and better ROI, ensuring that businesses get the most value from their marketing investments.

ALBERT.AI – PROS & CONS

Pros
Automates marketing tasks: Albert.ai can automate many marketing tasks, saving time and reducing human error. It can handle things like ad targeting, optimization, and analysis, leaving marketers more time to focus on strategy.
Personalization: Albert.ai uses machine learning to analyze customer behavior and preferences, creating more targeted and personalized marketing messages. This can lead to higher engagement and conversion rates.
Scalability: Albert.ai can handle large-scale campaigns with ease, making it ideal for businesses that need to reach a wide audience.
Real-time optimization: Albert.ai can adjust campaigns in real-time, making changes based on performance metrics. This can lead to more efficient spending and better ROI.

Data-driven insights: Albert.ai provides detailed performance metrics and analysis, allowing businesses to make data-driven decisions and optimize their marketing strategies.

Cons
Cost: Albert.ai is an expensive solution, and may not be feasible for smaller businesses with limited marketing budgets.
Complexity: Albert.ai is a complex system that requires significant setup and configuration. Businesses will need to invest time and resources into training and integration to get the most out of the platform.
Limited control: Because Albert.ai automates many marketing tasks, businesses may have less control over the details of their campaigns. Marketers will need to trust the AI to make the right decisions.
Dependence on data: Albert.ai relies heavily on data to make decisions, which means businesses will need to have access to high-quality data and keep it up to date.

TRADITIONAL MARKETING - PROS & CONS

Pros
Familiarity: Traditional marketing methods like print and radio advertising have been around for decades, and many businesses are familiar with how they work.
Control: Traditional marketing methods give businesses more control over their campaigns, including the message, design, and target audience.
Direct customer interaction: Traditional marketing methods can offer more direct customer interaction, such as in-store promotions or events.
Tangibility: Traditional marketing methods can create a physical, tangible presence for a brand, such as billboards or product displays.

Cons
Limited targeting: Traditional marketing methods often lack the targeting capabilities of digital marketing. They can reach a wide audience but may not be effective at reaching specific demographics or audiences.

Limited analytics: Traditional marketing methods provide limited performance metrics and analytics, making it harder to measure ROI and optimize campaigns.
Limited scalability: Traditional marketing methods can be expensive and time-consuming to scale up, making it harder to reach a large audience.
Declining effectiveness: Traditional marketing methods may not be as effective as they once were, as consumers increasingly turn to digital channels for information and entertainment.

While there are certainly some challenges to implementing Albert. ai, such as the cost and complexity of the system, the benefits are clear. By automating marketing tasks, providing personalized marketing messages, and offering real-time optimization, Albert.ai can help businesses increase marketing productivity and effectiveness, allowing them to better reach their target audiences and achieve their marketing goals. As more businesses turn to AI-powered marketing solutions, it's clear that Albert. ai can provide significant advantages over traditional marketing methods.

EXCELFORMULABOT.COM

Pros and Cons of using excelformulabot.com for business purposes compared to traditional ways of managing Excel formulas:

Pros	Cons
Saves time and reduces errors in formula creation	Dependence on internet connection
Provides instant formula recommendations and feedback	Dependence on third-party software and technology
Easy to use with a user-friendly interface	Requires additional cost for advanced features
Improves accuracy and consistency of formulas	Limited ability to customize or tailor to specific needs

Can improve productivity and efficiency in Excel use	Potential security concerns or data privacy risks

Using excelformulabot.com for business purposes has several advantages. One of the most significant benefits is the time and error reduction in formula creation. The bot provides instant formula recommendations and feedback, which can save a considerable amount of time and reduce the likelihood of errors in formula creation. Additionally, excelformulabot.com is easy to use, with a user-friendly interface that simplifies the process of managing Excel formulas.

Another advantage of excelformulabot.com is its ability to improve the accuracy and consistency of formulas. The bot's recommendations are based on data analysis, which can help ensure the accuracy and consistency of formulas. This can be particularly beneficial for businesses that rely heavily on Excel for financial analysis, forecasting, and other data-driven activities.

However, there are some potential drawbacks to using excelformulabot.com. One significant disadvantage is the dependence on an internet connection. The bot is cloud-based, which means that it requires an internet connection to function properly. This can be problematic for businesses with unreliable or slow internet connections.

Another potential issue with excelformulabot.com is the dependence on third-party software and technology. The bot requires integration with Excel, which may require additional software or technology. This can lead to compatibility issues or additional costs for advanced features. Additionally, excelformulabot.com has limited customization capabilities, which may be a drawback for businesses with specific formula needs.

Finally, there may be some security concerns or data privacy risks associated with using excelformulabot.com. As a cloud-based service, excelformulabot.com requires data to be stored off-site, which may be a concern for some businesses. It is essential to consider these potential risks and weigh them against the benefits of using the service.

Overall, excelformulabot.com can be an effective tool for businesses looking to improve productivity and efficiency in Excel use. Its ability to provide instant formula recommendations and feedback, improve accuracy and consistency, and save time makes it a valuable addition to any business's Excel toolkit. However, it is essential to consider the potential drawbacks, such as dependence on an internet connection and the need for additional software or technology, before making a decision.

JASPER.AI

Jasper.ai can be a valuable tool for businesses looking to increase their content creation capabilities. Compared to traditional methods of content creation, Jasper.ai can save time, reduce costs, and improve the quality and consistency of the output. With machine learning algorithms, the platform can generate high volumes of content quickly and efficiently, allowing businesses to scale their content creation efforts to meet growing demand.

In addition to increasing the speed and efficiency of content creation, Jasper.ai can also improve the quality and effectiveness of the content itself. With the ability to specify the desired tone, audience, and style of the content, businesses can ensure that their content aligns with their brand and meets their specific goals. Furthermore, the machine learning algorithms can analyze data to identify trends and patterns, which can be used to create more engaging and effective content that resonates with the target audience.

Another benefit of using Jasper.ai is its ability to customize the content creation process to the specific needs of a business. The platform allows users to choose from a variety of content types, including social media posts, email marketing campaigns, blog posts, and more. With this flexibility, businesses can create content that is tailored to their unique marketing strategy and goals.

Pros and Cons of Using Jasper.ai for Business Content Creation:

Pros:

- Saves Time: Jasper.ai can help businesses save time by automating the content creation process, allowing users to generate high-quality content quickly and efficiently.
- Improves Quality: The platform uses machine learning to generate content, which can improve the quality and consistency of the output, resulting in more engaging and effective content.
- Cost-Effective: Compared to traditional methods of content creation, Jasper.ai can be a more cost-effective solution, reducing the need for dedicated content creation staff.
- Customizable: Jasper.ai allows users to customize the content generation process by specifying the desired tone, audience, and style of the content.
- Scalable: The platform can easily scale to meet the content creation needs of businesses of all sizes, allowing them to create high volumes of content without sacrificing quality.

Cons:

- Limited Flexibility: Jasper.ai's content generation process is based on machine learning algorithms, which can limit the flexibility of the output. It may not be ideal for highly creative or complex content, such as design-heavy marketing materials.

- Lack of Control: While users can customize the content generation process to a degree, the machine learning algorithms ultimately control the output. This can lead to some lack of control or unpredictability in the result.
- Requires Learning Curve: Jasper.ai requires some learning to get the best results from the platform, which may take time for users to fully understand how to use it.
- Limited Customization: Although Jasper.ai allows for some customization of content, it may not meet the specific needs of a business's branding or unique style.
- Dependent on AI: As with any AI-based system, Jasper.ai's effectiveness is dependent on the quality of its machine learning algorithms and data input.

Overall, Jasper.ai can be a valuable tool for businesses looking to increase their content creation capabilities and improve the quality and effectiveness of their output. While it may not be the best solution for all types of content or businesses, particularly those that require a high degree of customization or flexibility, it can be a powerful asset for businesses that want to streamline their content creation process and improve their marketing efforts.

PROMO.AI

Implementing Promo.ai into a business can be an excellent way to increase engagement and improve the impact of newsletters compared to traditional newsletter methods. Promo.ai uses artificial intelligence to create personalized and targeted newsletters that are tailored to each individual recipient. This can lead to higher open and click-through rates, as customers are more likely to engage with content that is relevant to their interests.

One of the most significant advantages of Promo.ai is its time-saving capabilities. The platform offers pre-made templates and customizable content, which can speed up the newsletter creation process. This can be a huge time-saver for businesses that need to create newsletters regularly, freeing up more time for other marketing initiatives. With Promo.ai, businesses can create high-quality newsletters quickly and efficiently, without sacrificing quality.

Another significant benefit of Promo.ai is its data-driven insights. By analyzing customer behavior and preferences, Promo.ai can provide detailed performance metrics and analysis, allowing businesses to make data-driven decisions and optimize their email marketing strategies. This can lead to more efficient spending and better ROI, ensuring that businesses get the most value from their marketing investments.

PROMO.AI – PROS & CONS

Pros
Timesaving: Promo.ai can save time and effort compared to creating newsletters from scratch. The platform offers pre-made templates and customizable content, which can speed up the newsletter creation process.
Personalization: Promo.ai uses AI to analyze customer behavior and preferences, creating more targeted and personalized newsletters. This can lead to higher engagement and open rates.
Scalability: Promo.ai can handle large email lists, making it ideal for businesses that need to reach a wide audience.
Data-driven insights: Promo.ai provides detailed performance metrics and analysis, allowing businesses to make data-driven decisions and optimize their email marketing strategies.
Cost-effective: Promo.ai offers affordable pricing plans, making it accessible to small and medium-sized businesses with limited marketing budgets.

DANIEL DESTA

Cons
Limited control: Because Promo.ai uses pre-made templates and customizable content, businesses may have less control over the details of their newsletters. Marketers will need to trust the AI to make the right decisions.
Dependence on data: Promo.ai relies heavily on data to make decisions, which means businesses will need to have access to high-quality data and keep it up to date.
Limited design options: Promo.ai offers pre-made templates, but businesses may find the design options limited compared to creating newsletters from scratch.
Learning curve: Promo.ai is a new technology, and businesses will need to invest time and resources into training and integration to get the most out of the platform.

TRADITIONAL WAY – PROS & CONS

Pros
Control: Traditional newsletters give businesses more control over their content and design, allowing them to create a unique and customized newsletter that aligns with their brand.
Direct customer interaction: Traditional newsletters can offer more direct customer interaction, such as feedback and responses to the newsletter content.
Tangibility: Traditional newsletters can create a physical, tangible presence for a brand, such as in-store newsletters or mailers.

Cons
Time-consuming: Creating traditional newsletters from scratch can be time-consuming and may require significant resources to design and distribute.
Limited scalability: Traditional newsletters can be expensive and time-consuming to scale up, making it harder to reach a large audience.
Limited personalization: Traditional newsletters may not be as effective at personalizing content compared to AI-powered platforms like Promo.ai.
Limited data and analysis: Traditional newsletters may not provide detailed performance metrics and analytics, making it harder to measure ROI and optimize campaigns.

50

Furthermore, Promo.ai's scalability can help businesses reach a wider audience. With the platform's ability to handle large email lists, businesses can easily and quickly send newsletters to many recipients, helping to increase brand awareness and engagement. Additionally, the customizable content and pre-made templates can help businesses create newsletters that align with their brand and messaging.

While there are some challenges to implementing Promo.ai, such as the learning curve and dependence on data, the benefits are clear. By using artificial intelligence to create personalized and targeted newsletters, businesses can increase engagement and improve the impact of their newsletters, leading to higher open and click-through rates. With time-saving capabilities, data-driven insights, and scalability, Promo.ai can be an excellent addition to a business's email marketing strategy.

SURFERSEO.COM

Implementing SurferSEO.com into a business can provide numerous benefits for improving SEO and increasing website traffic. Traditional methods of SEO, such as manual keyword research, content analysis, and backlink building, can be time-consuming and require significant expertise. SurferSEO.com automates many of these processes and provides businesses with data-driven recommendations based on analysis of top-performing websites in their niche or industry. This can save businesses significant time and resources, while also improving the effectiveness of their SEO strategies.

In addition to time-saving benefits, SurferSEO.com provides a comprehensive analysis of a website's SEO, including keyword research, content analysis, and backlink analysis. This can help businesses identify areas for improvement and optimize their website for search engines, leading to increased rankings and traffic. By providing data-driven recommendations, SurferSEO.com can also help businesses make informed decisions about their SEO strategies and increase their chances of success.

One of the unique benefits of SurferSEO.com is its user-friendliness. Unlike traditional SEO methods that require technical expertise, SurferSEO.com is accessible to businesses of all sizes and industries. This means that even small businesses with limited marketing budgets can benefit from the platform's insights and recommendations.

Pros and Cons of using surferseo.com for business purposes compared to traditional ways of generating traffic and SEO:

Pros of SurferSEO.com:

- Comprehensive SEO analysis: SurferSEO.com provides a comprehensive analysis of a website's SEO, including keyword research, content analysis, backlink analysis, and more. This can help businesses optimize their website for search engines and improve their rankings.

- Data-driven recommendations: SurferSEO.com uses data-driven recommendations based on analysis of top-performing websites in the same niche or industry. This can help businesses make informed decisions about their SEO strategy and increase their chances of success.

- Timesaving: SurferSEO.com can save businesses a significant amount of time compared to traditional SEO methods. The platform automates many aspects of the SEO analysis and optimization process, allowing businesses to focus on other areas of their business.

- User-friendly: SurferSEO.com is user-friendly and doesn't require technical expertise to use. This makes it accessible to businesses of all sizes and industries.

Cons of SurferSEO.com:

- Cost: SurferSEO.com can be costly for some businesses, especially small businesses or those with limited marketing budgets.

- Limited customization: SurferSEO.com is based on a standardized methodology, so it may not be as effective for businesses with unique needs or requirements.

- Overreliance on data: While data-driven recommendations can be helpful, overreliance on data can sometimes lead to a lack of creativity and innovation in SEO strategies.

- No guaranteed results: While SurferSEO.com can provide valuable insights and recommendations, there are no guarantees that a business will see improved SEO rankings or increased traffic to their website.

Overall, SurferSEO.com can be a valuable tool for businesses looking to improve their SEO and drive traffic to their website. While it may not be the best solution for all businesses, particularly those with unique needs or limited budgets, it can provide comprehensive, data-driven insights and save time in the SEO optimization process.

While there are some potential drawbacks to SurferSEO.com, such as its cost and limited customization, the benefits of the platform make it a valuable tool for businesses looking to improve their SEO and drive traffic to their website. By implementing SurferSEO.com, businesses can improve the effectiveness of their SEO strategies, save time and resources, and make informed decisions about their digital marketing efforts.

www.ingramcontent.com/pod-product-compliance
Lightning Source LLC
LaVergne TN
LVHW051615050326
832903LV00033B/4516